THE GOLDEN YEARS

Living in a Retirement Center

by

Byron Oberst M.D., FAAP

www.trafford.com

North America & international
toll-free: 1 888 232 4444 (USA & Canada)
fax: 812 355 4082

DEDICATION

To the memory of my Beloved Mary

Who was the Epitome of a Wonderful Physician's Wife

The Angels came for her exactly on her Eighty-eighth Birthday, May 31, 2011

To my Sons: Byron, Terrance, and Mathew and their lovely wives

To my special Grandsons: Matthew, Justin, and Conor and their Wives

My Great Grandchildren: John, Annabelle, Sam, and Penelope Rose

A special thanks to my son, Matthew, whose computer expertise saved my bacon many times.

Mary and Obie

ACKNOWLEDGEMENTS

To my Beloved Mary who was my anchor and helpmate throughout our lifetime together. For sixty-six years, she was my stabilizing force. The magic in her hands was first felt when she grasped my hand on our initial date as we walked off the dance floor at the conclusion of the first set of music at beautiful Peony Park. This magic was present all through our lifetime together. I was a very fortunate man

To my Second Son, Terrance, who wielded his red editing pencil with great gusto and with unparalleled glee.

Books by B.B. Oberst M.D., FAAP

Practical Guidance for Pediatric and Adolescent Practice

Computer Applications to Pediatric Practice – A Primer

Co-Editor: R. Reid M.D.

Computers in Private Practice Management

Co-Author: J. Long PhD

Reflections on Pediatric Medicine from 1943 to 2010
     A True Dual Love Story

A Tale of a Mother, Her Three Sons, and Their Dog
     A Love Story of a Father for His Family

Miracles and Other Unusual Medical Experiences

Brownie Bill in Healthland
     Artist: Wilford E. Shook
A book for two to seven year olds to explain Body Defense Mechanisms

TABLE OF CONTENTS

PROLOGUE

This story will conclude the romance of the century which was written about in detail in my three books of my medical trilogy and which were recently published. The magic in Mary's hands began on our first date and lasted all through our lifetime of sixty-six years together until the angels came when she took her last breath.

Where do I begin with this current tale? "Let me start at that one moment in time which changed our lives forever". I'll describe the situation where my Beloved Mary fell at her Rheumatologist's office. She had endured a rheumatic arthritis condition after an anaphylactic reaction to the antibiotic "Cipro". Over time, the adverse effects of her arthritis deformed her left hand into a claw like appendage limiting her use of it. It was necessary for me to pick up the slack and attend to her needs by cutting up her food, opening twisting caps, and similar tasks. She seldom complained except occasionally saying, "I hurt". This assistance was not considered a burden, but a privilege for me to help her with her needs.

This catastrophe began while she was waiting at the curb at the doctor's office for me to bring the car to her on December 2010. As I was opening the car door, she cried out "Catch me"! I wasn't able to get to her in time. Whether this fall was due to a Transit Ischemic Arterial Spasm [TIA] or a minor stroke, I'll never know. I just know that our life underwent a dramatic change at that moment on that fateful day.

As I previously have had much trouble with my knees, I could not get down to assist my Helpmate. In a panic, I called for help from the doctor's office. Many workers answered my call. Someone called for the Rescue Squad. They were there within minutes – if not sooner. I wanted my Beloved to go to Methodist Hospital, but the Squad said that St. Joseph's Hospital was the Trauma Center "On Call" that day. Off my Beloved went without me. I immediately called my son, Matthew, and informed him about the situation. He would meet me at St Joe Hospital.

It was noon time, and there was so much traffic on the streets. I thought that I would never arrive at the hospital. The trip seemed to me it was lasting forever. It took me over thirty minutes, which without heavy traffic, would ordinarily take about fifteen. By the time I arrived at the hospital a full blown panic attack was residing in my heart. Being a doctor, the worst case scenarios kept coming to the fore in my mind.

Matt met me at the entrance and told me that my Beloved Mary was undergoing all kinds of tests including a brain scan. All, I could do was wait, fret, and worry. These circumstances were not an ideal situation for a doctor to have to endure when one's medical mind is filled with all sorts of horrendous images.

Finally, a professional person emerged and told me that my Beloved Mary was awake and doing well. All of her tests were OK so far including skull x-rays and a CAT Scan. They wanted to keep her overnight and run more tests on the morrow.

I quickly vetoed that suggestion and told the authorities that I wanted to transfer her to Methodist Hospital where all of her own physicians were on staff, and it was much easier for me to travel to Methodist to visit. They agreed. The transfer was arranged for without incident. It was about 7:30 pm when we finally were placed in a room at Methodist and were exhausted from that lengthy traumatic day.

Her Internist, Dr. Giitter, and Orthopedist, Dr. Robert. Cochran, examined my Beloved Mary and recommended the various aspects of her rehab program and whatever other tests were deemed necessary. This program was started immediately.

Later on, I was informed by the Methodist Staff about the need to investigate a long term Skilled Nursing Unit with Rehab facilities. They gave me a list of entities to check, which I did, Pronto.

Most of the facilities on the list, which I visited, were rather depressing until I walked in the Lakeside Village Complex. It was like receiving a breath of fresh air. The staff was very friendly. As I toured the facilities, it seemed more like a four star Resort Hotel than a retirement community. The surrounding grounds were expansive and encompassed massive beds of colorful flowers, and there was an accompanying extensive well manicured lawn. In some ways, it was breathtaking in its loveliness. Immediately, if not sooner, I knew that this was the place for my Beloved Mary to convalesce, to recover, and probably to live.

I gave them a deposit. There was available a large two bed room in the Skilled Nursing Area. I knew that I subsequently would need help with an Assisted Living place for the long run; and so we went onto the waiting list for this type of unit. As soon as possible, Mary was transferred to the Lighthouse section of the Lakeside Village from Methodist Hospital.

The Lakeside Village had all types of useful features which could accommodate a person's needs from an independent living apartment, a skilled nursing and rehab area, an assisted living area, and a memory unit, The Village had a very sophisticated wellness facility plus an indoor heated pool. All of these facilities were under one roof, which in itself made the total complex much more desirable than others that I had visited. A lovely lady, Lynnie, gave me a tour of the premises. It was very enlightening and made the decision much easier as to where we would live in the near future, and so it came to pass.

My son, Matthew, and I attended the first evaluation Conference concerning my Beloved Mary. Whew! What an eye opener and enlightenment this conference ended up being. A feisty, small, Physical Therapist, Kelly Fairfield, stated that Mary would need about three months of therapy. "What! Why so long"?, I asked. Kelly very firmly and pleasantly answered, "Do you want her to walk again or have her live permanently in a wheelchair"? There could be only one reply, "She stays however long necessary".

Matt agreed with me. This decision changed my own medical time frame, "Big Time". I had planned to have my right knee replaced during the spring. I immediately, made plans with Dr. Cochran's office to have it done as soon as possible. The Lighthouse folks said that I could rehab in Mary's room as there was sufficient space for a second bed. We would be together. The nights were long and empty without her cheery voice in our Regency Apartment.

In the light of these unexpected developments, I talked with the Rental Office at Lakeside to see if we could improvise and utilize an Independent Apartment during the ensuing interval until an Assisted Living Unit became available. The Immanuel people were very accommodating. Fortunately, an Independent Unit was immediately available. Over time, several Assisted Living Units became available, but we turned them down. Mary was doing so well that we stayed in our apartment.

Plans were made by Matt, which included the highly recommended "Denise's Senior Moving Services", to move our apartment contents from our Regency Apartment during the time that my knee was being repaired in Methodist Hospital; and so It came to pass without a hitch. Denise's group did a spectacular job without me supervising.

CHAPTER 1

A New Life Beginning at Lakeside Village

At long last, we arrived at our destination at Methodist Hospital about 8:30 pm. It had been a very long and eventful day. A day of surprises that we had not foreseen when we left our house about 9:30 am that same morning. My Beloved Mary had sustained fractures of her cute little nose, upper left humerus [arm], and left wrist. As she had fallen flat on her face, both eyes and facial features were black and blue. She looked like a raccoon with both eyes being so discolored. She had the appearance as though she had gone about five rounds with Joe Louis and came out on the short end of things.

Early the next morning, her rehab at Methodist Hospital began in earnest and continued throughout the next several days. As I said, I was informed that she would need some long term work; so that I had better start looking at for some useful living facilities. The rehab staff gave me a list of recommended places.

I settled on the Immanuel Lakeside Village. The staff was so friendly and accommodating. Back to Methodist Hospital, I went and told them of my desires. They made accommodations for Mary to be transferred that same day and fortunately there was a large room available in the Village Skilled Nursing Rehab Unit. As my Beloved Mary was deemed ready for the transfer, off we went in an ambulance service to our future destiny; this ride left much to be desired as to comfort and ease. We hit every bump and pot hole in route to Lakeside whether by happenstance or with deliberation. It was obvious that the ambulance's shocks were caput. At the end of the ride, I checked my teeth to be sure they all were intact. This ride played hob with Mary's back problems. Previously, she had sustained several impacted vertebrae. She was tucked into her new quarters with a minimum of fuss.

I would call Mary every morning before she had breakfast and at night after she was ready for bed. It was so lonesome without her upbeat presence around our Regency Apartment. As it was going to be quite awhile before an Assisted Living Unit would be available, I settled on utilizing an Independent Unit until the other would become available. Ours was a two bedroom unit on the third floor up with the "Elite". I would take good care of her, I promised myself.

The news of my Beloved Mary's need of three months of rehab work had rearranged my own plans. I had planned to have my right knee replaced later that spring when Mary was much improved and in the Assisted Living area. If my surgery could be accomplished pronto; then, we could rehab together as Mary's room would easily accommodate two hospital beds.

Dr. Robert Cochran, an old patient of mine since birth, was my Orthopedist as well as Mary's . He would perform my surgery; thus, It came to pass without any complications. This was my first ever surgery, and the folks at Methodist couldn't believe it. If I was asked once, I was asked at least ten times if this were true as if I was some freak or other at the tender age of eighty-nine and no previous surgery.

The Lighthouse folks agreed that I could rehab in Mary's room. We would be together. A second bed was installed. The nights had been long and empty without her sweet voice in our Regency Apartment.

My knee surgery was uneventful. After beginning my rehab work at Methodist, I moved to Lakeside Village and the Lighthouse. My Beloved Mary was once again by my side. The nursing personnel said that she began sleeping better with me in her room. How gratifying for me to know that she needed me to be near her.

My rehab went along very well under the vicious and demanding eye of Kelly Fairfield without any remissions. My progress was very good. In fact, it was better than anyone anticipated for an old duffer. At last, I was cleared by the Occupational Therapist as being able to put on my socks, shoes, and to get in and out of my car.

The time came for me to go home to our independent apartment; and so I did. It was great to be home. I would go to the Lighthouse to have lunch and supper with my Beloved Mary. We would visit and while away the hours kibitzing and reading books or magazines like newlyweds. Our meals were enjoyable and enlivened by many interesting folks. There was Blanche, who had been an Army Nurse and had been in the Battle of the Bulge and saw Dachau amongst other adventures during World War II. She related some fascinating stories over our supper hour. Each night, I would ask her, "What is out history lesson for tonight". She obliged us on more than one occasion.

The apartment contents were moved and aligned as I had previously indicated on a floor plan of the apartment before my surgery. The floor plan was supplied by the Rental Office. The unit was on the third floor with all of the "Elite in their fancy apartments" overlooking the parking lot. Our unit consisted of two bedrooms, a complete, but small, kitchen, two bathrooms, living room, and an inviting porch. The apartment contained about twelve hundred square foot of space. It was about the same size as our Regency Apartment. There was considerable landscaping to be seen from our porch, including a massive bed of ever blooming rose bushes to mask the unsightly parking area.

These living quarters were more than adequate for our needs. We were very comfortable with this arrangement. This facility came with the laundering of our bath towels each week, and the apartment was cleaned every two weeks. One of the better features of this cleaning service for me was that the house keeping folks changed and laundered the bed sheets with each visit. Hurrah and Halleluiah! I really disliked having to change the sheets "Big Time"!

Before my knee surgery, I would have supper at the Lighthouse with Mary. I continued to do so after my rehab was completed and I had moved into our third floor apartment. It was so nice to be surrounded by all our familiar pictures, objects, and furniture. We did not have to dispose of much excess contents from our Regency Apartment. Most of our things were accommodated very easily.

When it was time for Mary to move back to our apartment, our oldest son, Byron, and his lovely wife, Shirley, came from Oregon to help. What a delightful homecoming this event was. My beloved Mary directed traffic from her royal throne concerning all of the adjustments she desired with the apartment furniture. By and Shirley did the moving of the various requests by the directing Major Domo. In true womanly fashion, these adjustments were made time and again, here, there, and back again until everything was just perfect. It finally satisfied "The Little General's" taste. I just sat in a corner and nodded fine, and let the activities flow wherever they went. I knew that any of my suggestions would be vetoed or even ignored if they were given the courtesy of a consideration at all. My computer and office room was my sole domain and where I held sway. Our apartment resulted in a cozy and comfortable place in which to reside with a minimum of hassle.

Mary and I quickly fell into a comfortable daily routine. After I helped her get dressed in the mornings, we would have tea and read the paper; then, we would have breakfast in the apartment consisting of cold cereal and milk. I would go to the Wellness Center each Monday. Wednesday, and Friday about 11:00 am for my own exercise program. Mary would go to the Center every Tuesday and

Thursday at 11:00 am. On the way back to our apartment, I would stop in the dining room for my Beloved Mary's favorite "BLT" and a half of some other type of sandwich for me. Our lunches were not very large.

The evening meal was served from 4:30 to 6:00 pm. We would journey to the dining room where the Maître 'd would seat us with different folks. This procedure was a nice way to meet and become acquainted with various people. One of the special features about living at the Lakeside Village was that they employed such wonderful teenagers to serve us dinner.

These young people were a real delight. As we became more acquainted and in my usual nosey manner from my Adolescent Practice days, I would ask about their school activities and future thoughts about careers. The students were above average in abilities and were involved in many different school activities from Student Council, playing leads in their school musicals, and into sports. They were a breath of fresh air.

One of the young ladies, Nikkie, was in Nurse's Training. She was a CME, and worked in another place. She was a server in her spare time from her other duties because she enjoyed being around we older folks. I would frequently give her pop quizzes on different aspects of her anatomy courses. For example, "Name the "bones of the legs". She enjoyed this game we played; and so did her parents. I hoped that this would help her with her course. Another young lady thought she wanted to be a Neurosurgeon, and several others wanted to go into nursing,

One of our favorite dinner companions was Bea A. She was a bright and articulate Jewish lady, who would regale us with stories of her trips to Israel and Rome. She was a great story teller. She was a very staunch Democrat, and we would enjoy a friendly tiff over different items of the political spectrum. I really liked her.

There was a slender, pixie-like fellow, who had a perpetual twinkle in his eye, whose wife, Dottie, was in the Lighthouse when we were there. We usually ate dinner with her and several others while we were in the Lighthouse. He was a great tease. He and I became friends and joshed with each other frequently. This acquaintance blossomed into a real friendship.

My Beloved Mary continued her rehab work at the Wellness Center with the Director, Pretty Henny Penny. Penny never walked anywhere, she galloped. Mary thoroughly enjoyed her. They would laugh and giggle like a pair of teenagers. Any actual physical rehab activity seemed purely coincidental. Mary made great progress with her walking utilizing a walker. It was so heart warming to see her come out her reclusive shell that she had acquired at Regency due the lack of any social interactions. My Beloved Mary literally blossomed like a rose. It was so gratifying to observe her wonderful personality flower once again. Her general health greatly improved even though she was still very frail physically.

The nice thing about the Lakeside Village was that so many amenities are conveniently available within its walls. For some unknown and unexplained reason, ladies love to go to the beauty parlor even though it does not seem necessary when you look at their general appearance. Mary was no exception. When we lived at Regency, I would wash her hair before taking her to her stylist of some thirty years. My Beloved Mary had a bad back with many painful fractured and impacted vertebrae. The trip to the beauty pallor was quite a painful and exhausting feat; thus the necessity for the washing of her hair at home. At Lakeside, she would just need to go a short distance to the beauty salon on the first floor. Sherrie was so kind and considerate of my Beloved Mary. She was able to wash Mary's hair in her shop with a minimum of difficulty; so I lost another job. Shucks! The transition from Sue to Sherrie went without a hitch. We went every other Wednesday. I gave up my barber of some thirty years because of the convenience Sherrie offered. She would trim my few twigs at regular intervals whenever my tonsorial head covering became unsightly. Where all that cut hair came from I'll never know. It didn't seem to reside on t he top of my head that is for sure.

CHAPTER 2.

"Just Call Me Joe"

As I was making our beds in the morning, Mary would never tolerate me just throwing the covers back and calling it made. She would sit in her rocker supervising and religiously studying the paper each morning while I performed my morning chores. When I would cast an eye towards her while she was so occupied and she reminded me of the painting of "Whistler's Mother. I fondly recall those moments, today, as I still make my bed every morning. I can almost see her sitting there avidly reading the paper wearing her silly white bed hat and keeping an eye on me to be sure the bed is made properly. I know that I am being facetious, but it seems so real in my mind's eye.

Just Call Me "Joe"

Over time, we ate supper with many different people. One of these folks was a fellow named Joe, just "Call me Joe". He is a small framed person with a pixie like appearance and a bright, saucy twinkling in his eyes. He has deep blue eyes and extremely white hair, what there is of it. He combs it over from left to right. Ha!

He has had such a life filled with so many different adventures. He Lived in North Omaha near 24th and Ames near the Fire Station where he played on the grounds extensively.

He went to Saratoga Grade School and North High School. He graduated after me. He told me the story of being on the stage crew high up in the wings during a high school production when he decided to play a trick on a fellow classmate by dropping a water filled balloon on this classmate as he walked beneath him. The balloon was launched. OOOOPs!! The balloon landed dead center on the Principle's head as he walked under the space instead of his designated victim. He still owes North High School some ninety hours of after school punishment. He hopes that the Statute of Limitations has run out by now. Wishful thinking! He was an experienced "Roller Blade Dancer". Wow!

Early on, he had many odd jobs including a paper route. He traded a year of newspapers for flying lessons at The Burnham Flying School at the Epply Airport. He helped around the Omaha Ice and Cold Storage Plant. He even assisted in delivering ice with some of the most interesting experiences. He ended up being a person of many facets and varied talents. An amazing man!

He used his brother's birth certificate to enroll in the Navy Flight School as he was underage. He had a fascinating background during World War II. He was a Navy flyer and flew off of twenty-seven different aircraft carriers. His longest time aboard any one carrier was eight months. At times, he flew off those tiny "Jeep Carriers, which supplied replacement planes and pilot reinforcements to the big operational Carriers.

He was in the battles of the New Hebrides Islands and the Philippine Sea Straits. He flew fighter protection at the Battle of Okinawa. He relates how clouds were a pilot's best friend as one could lose a pursuing Jap plane in their fleecy white bodies.

A line of ships [Two Carriers, Battle Ships, several Cruisers, and many Destroyers] went in a single file one night through the Philippines Straits with "Lights Out" and the "Smoking Lamp Out". The entire entourage was in a stealth mode. The ships had a pre-determined course which mandated turning directions exactly at certain spots on compass headings. If the turn was NOT precise, the ship was deemed to be an enemy vessel and was treated accordingly. Ipso facto, those instructions were followed to the exact letter.

In one occasion, he was shot down 300 miles from his carrier. It was imperative if one had to ditch a plane in the ocean that the nose off the plane be kept upward when landing so that the plane would not somersault. He floated in a life raft for an unknown space of time before he was picked up by an American Submarine. He stayed aboard the sub for two weeks before coming into port. Fortunately, the life raft was equipped with a small bottle of water and some food. There was stored aboard a funnel shaped device to catch the rains which frequently came during the afternoons.

On another occasion, his plane was on fire and out of ammunition. He had to bail out over Truk Island {a major fortified Japanese bastion in the Pacific]. It was imperative **NOT** to open the parachute until one was about one thousand feet from the ground. In this manner, Japanese pilots would have a harder time locating their victim and machine gunning him while he was dangling in the air. He landed in a tree. An Island Watcher discovered him, cut him down, and hid him in a cave for three [3] day.

For food learned on a survival course, he ate fuzzy grub worms, which were roasted over a fire. Ugh! He claims that they were not too bad. He was rescued by a Navy PT Boat after hiding on the island.

On an additional occasion, he crash landed aboard his carrier because his plane tail hook had been shot off. The tail hook was supposed to curtail his forward progress by catching a metal rope while landing before running into the deck crash barriers. As a consequence, his plane ran through the first barrier and crashed into the second one. His plane was a total wreck and was tossed over the ship's side. The flight deck folks had to cut him out of the plane within a very few minutes. Clearance speed was essential as following planes had to land and needed an unobstructed landing area.

He hurt his back with this crash which still gives him trouble. At the same time, he sustained a bad concussion. Oh My! As a result of these injuries, he was re-assigned to Submarine Patrol and Search and Rescue duty out of Alaska and flew a large multi-motor seaplane. They picked up many downed fliers. His back gives him trouble still in today's world, but he is alive and enjoys tormenting me with gusto. We have become very good friends.

While on this new assignment in Alaska and on one occasion, he flew supplies to Antarctica. The motors and propellers of their plane needed to be kept turning while on the ground as it was fifty degrees plus below zero. If the motors were turned off, they would not start again in that severe cold. They were on the ground less than thirty minutes and, then, off again with a big sigh of relief.

He was the "Con Officer" aboard the Carriers and monitored the many poker games aboard. These games were frequently held in the eight "Flight Ready Rooms". Naturally, this task required the necessity of taking his cut of every pot. He was what some folks might classify as a "Real Operator"!

After the War, he went to Iowa State University and lived in a boarding house with fifteen other students. He obtained a degree in Electrical Engineering and another one in Electricity. Obviously, he is no dumbbell. Over time, he became a Master Electrician, Construction Estimator, and Foreman. He worked on many major projects in and around Omaha and outside of Nebraska .

He was working one very hot summer day on a high voltage line, his T-shirt was wet with sweat, and it touched the 14,000 Volt wire. Even though he was wearing thick, heavy, rubber gloves, he was thrown backward into a cement wall. As a result, when his hair grew back, it was dead white and no curl. Ouch! After the War, he was a small plane pilot and owner of many different planes along with his first wife, who was a triplet. He bought, refurbished, and sold many types of planes. His first wife passed away due to a form of cancer. How sad!

Miscellaneous Endeavors

He has been a Volunteer Fireman and became a trained EMT while living near Broken Bow, Nebraska. He learned to scuba dive to aid the Department. His first wife inherited part of a ranch in Western Nebraska . He imagined big ideas and tried to pretend that he was a Cowboy with a large Stetson hat and leather chaps. To prove his cowboy status, he competed in a rodeo bulldogging steers contest. He went after three steers; and consequently, ate considerable amount of dirt and whatever else was in it. He dusted off his hands and hung up his spurs and chaps for a more reasonable pastime. He no longer wanted to be a "Rootin Tooting Shooting" cowboy.

He was an Entrepreneur par Excellence" and ran an Appliance TV store while living in the West. He successfully sold many ranchers TV sets. He assembled a converted truck mobile unit with which to install a reception tower for the TV sets that he sold to the ranch owner.

His work was guaranteed. He relates how a rancher called and complained that his brand new TV set wouldn't work. Old "Joe" made a house call. While evaluating the reasons why the TV didn't work, he noticed that the set was **NOT** plugged into the outlet. Oh my! The rancher was chagrined, and Old "Joe" was a happy man.

Later in life, he bought, restored small houses, and resold them. At one time, he owned twenty small houses as rental property. He owned several small apartment buildings and a small shopping mall. The administrative work and associated frustrations of maintenance became of major concern. He sold his properties and retired from being a landlord.

For awhile, he was a Federal Arson Investigator. He was, especially, tough when inspecting restaurant kitchens for fire hazards because of the accumulated grease in the stove fans. As an inspector, he relates that from the fire accelerants put into the gasoline there can be identified where the product was purchased as each station adds its own materials. Amazing!

His first wife, who passed away from a malignancy, insisted that she learn to fly and had her own plane. They flew many different places and enjoyed life to its fullest.

He met his second wife at a bereavement session and relates how he was able to get into her good graces by feeding her small dog " Doggie Treats". Boy! What an operator. He took dance lessons, which he badly needed. He and his wife went dancing several times a week.

He loved fishing and flew to Alaska and Canada over a weekend on many occasions. He was a hunter of deer, elk, moose, and caribou. He is a man for all seasons and is to be greatly admired for his versatility.

He joined a group of fellows to engage in Demolition Derbies. They determined the bumper system on the Cadillac's was the best for this endeavor. They were allowed to install "Roll Bars", but that was the only modification allowed to the cars. He states that he drove in at least eight Derbies and occasionally won. Pssst! I let him think that I believe him. Ha!

Today, he enjoys flying small remote control planes and helicopters. He built one plane from scratch with a wingspan of seven feet. On one occasion while he was flying a plane in his apartment, which was a **BIG No! NO!** The plane came within a gnat's hair of hitting the ceiling fire extinguisher. Although, he has a small pixie like build and appearance; he is tough as nails.

He voluntarily gave up his seat on a World War II Honor Flight for someone who was enfeebled and would not be able to wait for another chance to go. He is a very thoughtful man. In conclusion, I think that he is a very special person. He is a man for all seasons! Please, don't tell him that I said so!!!

Chapter 3

Discoveries

I was surprised to learn how many of the Village citizens were in their nineties and others at or near one hundred. Being a speculative and observing physician, this fact made me ponder as to the reasons for such longevity. I concluded the reason to be based up on these six [6] major factors.

1. Good and balanced nutritional food

2. Convenient planned and programmed regular exercises.

3. Accessible and congenial companionship for conversations and social interactions

4. A safe, secure, and esthetic appealing environment in which to live.

5. Convenient access to one's faith. Being a Catholic, I can go to Holy Communion every Sunday morning and to Holy Mass every Thursday afternoon. It is very essential to be able to conveniently practice one's faith, which is so critical for a satisfied and contented life. There are services for the other folks. This access is so much a part of the Immanuel Mission principles of Body, Mind, and Spirit.

6. Multiple Interactions with youthful people to intermix the ages and interests

There were a number of other discoveries which I made about the Village population that never ceased to amaze me such as:

The problem of hearing is readily apparent with the number of hearing aids being utilized. This is an obvious interesting medical fact for me.

It is with a great deal of wonderment to behold the many spouses, who are caring for their mate with Alzheimer's memory loss, macular degeneration, glaucoma, and/or cataracts. This group of patients is a windfall for the eyeball doctors [ophthalmologists and Hearing Specialists]. Their spouses were and are to be commended for their dedication.

Having had a touch of assisted living needs in caring for my Beloved Mary after her fall and rehabilitation, these spouses are rapidly earning their own crown in heaven. My Mary seldom complained about her disabilities. Occasionally, she would say, "I hurt", that was all.

Many spouses look after their soul mates until it becomes impossible to continue the care in their own apartment; then, the nearby Memory Unit or Assisted Living Area becomes a necessity or, maybe, even the use of the skilled nursing area..

The numbers of folks who have undergone corrective heart surgery or joint replacement are too numerous to count. These corrections constitute a boon to the carpenter bone doctors [Orthopedists] and or to the pump specialists [Cardiologists].

For a physician, this close-up experience has been both eye opening and very rewarding. It has been a period of true enlightenment for little old me.

Another useful assess is the nearby location of banks, grocery stores, gas stations, cleaners, and various and other sundry of stores offering a variety of necessities.

CHAPTER 4

The Barmores

After we moved into our apartment on the third floor, which I facetiously called it the penthouse area or nosebleed area, and being up with the "Elite". We had barely entered our apartment when there came a loud earth shaking and thundering pounding on the door. There stood Johnnie B. an old, old friend and fellow physician. He and his lovely wife, Dorothy, lived just down the hall from our domicile. They were married August 5, 1945. We were married December 27, 1945. Quite a coincidence; thereafter, our lives soon become intricately intertwined forever more.

The Barmores

We were classmates, intern mates, and fellow residents together. He was in anesthesia, and I was in pediatrics. We were inducted into the Army Medical Corps at Brook Army Medical Center in San Antonio, Texas, at the same time. Both of our first born children were conceived while we were in San Antonio, Texas.

At Fort Sam Huston and the Brooke Army Medical Center, we received extensive training in what it takes to become an Army Doctor. This training included the many various and assorted duties connected with this position. The training was all encompassing from learning much more about venereal disease than I ever wanted to know, to barrack health, and the important all encompassing food sanitation needs. One way or another, during my army and medical practice life, most of this knowledge was utilized.

We were literally stuffed to overflowing with different bits of information for six weeks; and, then, we were sent forth into the cold, cruel world to sink or swim.   At the conclusion of our training, John was sent to Beaumont General Army Hospital in El Paso, Texas; and I was sent in a roundabout manner to Fort Dix, New Jersey with an unexpected and unwanted stop in New York City by the Army's mistake for six weeks. Ha! Ha! What a surprise! My many Fort Dix experiences, which were extensive, are reiterated in my first book, "Reflections on Pediatric Medicine fro 1943 to 2010".

The next year, we, both, ended in Japan. John, his lovely wife, Dorothy, and Ann Elizabeth, their firstborn, were in Yokohama at the big Army Hospital. My Beloved Mary and I were sent to Sendai, which was a town of about two hundred thousand inhabitants, and was located two hundred miles north of Tokyo. We traveled on telegraph orders for coordinated travel after much struggling with army red tape. Our oldest boy was six weeks old when we left the states. This town had been recently devastated by a Tsunami. I was at the 172nd Station Hospital, which was housed in a former cement built Insurance Building This building had survived the tremendous firebombing that destroyed most of this city during World War II.

We spent our Thanksgiving and Christmas Holidays with our dear friends. Byron, our first born, enjoyed bedeviling their Ann Elizabeth whenever we were together. He seemed to delight in pulling her hair and making her cry. The big bully! We served in the Occupation of Japan under General Douglas MacArthur. What a unique experience this was! We stayed with the Barmores on our way home while waiting for our ship, The S.S. Sergeant Freeman. This ship was a converted "Liberty Ship", which was hastily built during the War to carry supplies to the troops. It was an old "Rust Bucket" and was nothing like the luxury cruise liner on which we traveled to Japan.

After John and I finished our service time and had completed the remainder of our medical training in our respective specialties, we ended up in Omaha. I was privileged to be their family pediatrician. They had four children-two girls and two boys. Now, we are living down the hall from each other. What a legacy!

Dorothy was an only child. She grew up on a farm in Iowa. She and John met at a small college in mid Iowa. She was in an education program for becoming a teacher of English at the high school level. John was an only child and grew up on a ranch on the Niobrara River in the Sand hills country in Northwestern Nebraska. He rode his pony, "Shorty", to the country school. While living on the ranch, John could rope a steer by its hind legs. What a feat! He became a rootin, tootin, shootin, ropin cowboy. Man Oh Man! When he was in his big Stetson Hat, leather chaps, two holstered six shooters, and boots, he looked like a real, tough hombre.

When he was in high school, he repaired radios in his shop in town. While an intern, he was always putting something together in his room. He speaks of, "While haying on the ranch, he would try to make a ranch hand working on top of the haystack fall off". Such innocence! John was quite a trickster. When a fellow intern was in the shower and was all covered with soap, he would sneak into the utility room next door to the shower and turn off the water; then, after awhile, he would turn on only the cold water. Oh my! What a fuss and loud howls that created. After scurrying back to his room, he had the nerve to pretend to have no knowledge of this prank.

John became an excellent anesthesiologist. He did most of the anesthesia work for Dr. Delbert Neis, an outstanding cardiac and pulmonary surgeon. He worked at the University Med Center for a number of years and then, moved to the Methodist Hospital group. When the call for help would come, he would work any where needed.

When we started living at the Lakeside Village, the four of us would eat dinner together rather frequently. It was like having a member of the family close by. They, recently, moved to the Assisted Living section; so I visit them each Sunday after our own fancy Sunday brunch. Because of Dorothy's health they are about to move to the Skilled Nursing facility. This convenience is another dividend for living here. There daughter, Alice, does a yeoman's job in looking after her parents. As I write this missal, the angels just came for Dorothy. Another dear friend has departed this world on October 16, 2014.

Here at the Village, there are innumerable activities available to partake in if one is so inclined. I enjoy the monthly men's luncheon outings [Blue Brothers]. There are about ten fellows who travel to different restaurants around Omaha. When the ladies {Sammie, Lucy, and Maggie]} from the Activities Staff join us to drive the bus, it is a hoot! The fellows tease them without mercy; but they seem to enjoy these antics. Naturally, I do not indulge in such antics.

The Village driving service is especially helpful to assist folks in getting to their doctor appointments, to the grocery store, or to Wal-Mart, and other close-by businesses. Needed elective drop-offs are available on Fridays with a pick-up at this destination on the basis of a phone call. Now that I sold my car, I enjoy these features very much.

At periodic intervals, there are planned tours to different sites such as, the Werner Storm Chasers professional ballpark for a game, the Leid Lodge in Nebraska City for lunch, to the Nebraska City Mall where I purchased a beige long sleeved shirt and a light grey sweater at the Van Huesen Store. I thought the selections available were very poor. We traveled to the Nebraska Crossing Mall Outlet for browsing the many new stores near Gretna, Nebraska. There are tours of the city to see the many colorful, twinkling Christmas lights, and many other excursions including going to a small but expanding brewery. Here I enjoyed "Wheat Beer" for the first time. Though, I grew up on home brewed beer, in my later years, beer has had such a bitter taste and that it had no appeal for me until imbibing the "Wheat Beer". There is always something around here to see and be engaged in if one so desires. These Activity Ladies work very hard to provide different types of things for us to enjoy.

There are movies on Saturday and Sunday nights with a great big screen in the activities room. There are various types of entertainment on Wednesday evenings after dinner. For example, on Wednesday, April 23, 2014, my good friend, former golfing partner, and master magician, Wallie, gave a magic performance at 6:30 pm. It was great and was so very entertaining. After a number of years, he finally gave up on sawing his wife in half. There are frequently different musical types of offerings.

Each holiday has its own theme with specific colorful decorations and, celebrations. The worker bees and many inhabitants dress in costume according to the occasion. In the mid winter, there is a talent show with performances by the staff, our young high school servers, who exhibit great aptitudes, along with the inmates per Se. The Servers, Clarie and Fammy, are great piano virtuosos; Oliie is a skilled flutist, and "Hot Lips" Jake is a trumpet player in the cut of "Artie Shaw or Al Hirt". He plays in a swing band in high school amidst other musical groups. The talent show is not polished, but is loads of fun and, at times, contains exceptional talent. One of the fellows, Sonny Boy, that I eat supper with, plays the harmonica by ear very well and has many renditions for a wealth of music nonstop for the talent show.

I am not one to engage in many activities. My plate was too full for most of my life; so I just sit back and enjoy what appeals to me. I was volunteered, by the powers that be, and accepted a spot on the Village Foundation Committee, which mission is to provide a safety net for the people who have outlived their monies and would, otherwise, have to move. The point and purpose of this Foundation is to help people with their rent, to able to remain in their own homes, and to stay amidst their friends. This is a very worthwhile cause; thusly, I accepted and actively participate.

My major pastime, at this point in my long and colorful lifetime, is in writing books about my medical life experiences. These experiences were both unique from the ordinary run of the mill medical practices and was chocked full with the many unusual encounters, which were very extensive in many instances. I had previously published several technical medical books. Now, I have just completed writing a trilogy on my medical life. I am one of the few physicians still on the green side of the grass, who has lived through the vast and outstanding changes that medicine has undergone over the past seventy years during my own medical lifetime. The Trilogy consists of the following stories:

1. "Reflections on Pediatric Medicine from 1943 to 2010"

    This book describes how I witnessed the many faceted changes occurring in medicine starting with the introduction of Penicillin at the Med Center, when I was a Junior Medical Student, into the treatment armamentarium of physicians and all the other subsequent antibiotics which have been discovered. These medications changed the way a doctor could actually treat disease entities. There was the impact of immunizations on the health of children; my own pioneering efforts utilizing the exchange transfusion method the rH positive infant with a rH negative Mother in the treatment of this entity, handling the deplorable Attention Deficit Disorder with and without Hyperactivity; being a part of the beginnings of adolescent medicine, especially, from a private practice stance [here were not many practitioners interested in this age group early on]; engaging in the fascinating new world of computers in medicine; and the painful enduring of the introduction of health insurance into the office practice for better or worse. This phenomena greatly increased our office costs amidst many other generated vast headaches. It is an interesting chronology of the changes in medicine from then until now.

2. "A Mother, Her Three Sons, and their Dog"

This book is largely about my family and some about medicine. This book chronicles the immense impact of a busy, busy medical practice had on our family, and how we coped with its demands and remained an intact family entity. It is an interesting treatise on our active family life.

3. "Miracles and Other Unusual Medical Experiences"

I had two [2] real honest to goodness miracles during my medical lifetime. Neither of these patient should have survived let alone become truly functioning, intact adult citizens. Because of my unique training, army, and my humongous practice experiences, my medical life contained a number of fascinating cases, which most physicians never encounter. I recall a number of them in this tome.

These books are available through Amazon and Barnes and Noble on line or with a visit to the Barnes & Noble Customer Service Desk. They need to be ordered on a print on demand basis. The turn around time is very short for ordering any of these books. The cost factors are quite reasonable; so far my royalties have been miniscule.

CHAPTER 5

Old Harry
The Ideal Citizen

I want to write a few more words about Tom, Dick, and Harry. Obviously, these names are aliases of fellows that I have met here at the Lakeside Village and admire greatly. Their stories will be scattered throughout this missal. Harry grew up in a small town in outstate Nebraska with a population of about seven hundred.

"Old Harry"

How He survived a Wife, Five Daughters, Four Sons, and being Mayor of Small Town, Nebraska Seven Times WOW!

A Man of Many Hats

As an aside, watch your billfold and hold on tight as he is a vicious pinochle player with no holds barred. He has a pleasant, kindly grandfatherly face, and a pleasant sonorous voice that grasps your attention whenever he utters a word. He has a kind and friendly appearance with a twinkle in his eyes. His general ambiance instills and demands your confidence; so watch out! He is not a small built person, but is a very nice one.

Early Life:

He graduated from High School in 1944 from a small town near Dodge, Nebraska and grew up on a farm having considerable duties assigned relating to the chickens, egg production, and egg classification. He joined the Army in World War II, but was discharged on the death of his father in order to become the breadwinner in the family.

He was on one of the "Honor Fights" of World War II veterans who visited the special War Memorial and others in Washington D C.

He drove a Gas Truck for the local Farmer's Union from 1945 to 1959. He was married in this small town in Nebraska, in September 1948. He and his lovely wife, subsequently, had nine children. Oh My! So many mouths to feed, educate, and daughters to marry.

He was the pitcher and manager of the local baseball team and at one time pitched a "No Hitter" against Hooper, Nebraska; so he says. He coached Midget and American Legion Ball Teams. His teams won the State Title in the Class B category in 1965 and again in 1972.

Middle Life in Small Town, Nebraska:

He went into the Insurance Business on a part time basis before 1959. Later, he became the Sales Representative and manager of a major life Insurance agency in 1959. His Agency was named the top Agency in 1964. He became the Company's Area Manager for East Central Nebraska in 1967, and he trained twenty-five new salesmen in twenty-one different counties.

He was a volunteer fireman for thirteen years. The first volunteer to arrive at the fire station was the one who was designated to drive the truck; thus, the incentive was to arrive at the station as early as possible. Old Harry did not drive the truck very often. Oh Shucks!

While he lived in Small Town, Nebraska:

He was on the Village Board from 1961-1977 and was Mayor of this community for seven terms. He, obviously, had a great and effective political machine. He introduced many town improvements such as:

1. Hard street curbs

2. A city swimming poll

3. He gathered folks together to plan, build, and manage a local "Nursing Facility", which is still a functioning unit, and remains under local control. He was a great administrator.

He sat in many different civic seats over a vast expanse of time. He was a member of the Chamber of Commerce and was the secretary of the Dodge Development Corporation. He was the Commander of the local chapter of the American Legion. The chapter needed a body so he was it. He was an active member of the local Catholic Church and was a Board Member of the Francis Howard Hospital Foundation for twenty years

Life in the Insurance Business: Oh Boy!!

He was in Insurance Sales for forty-five years. He bought a building for his agency. He was a member of his company's One Hundred Million and Two Hundred Million Dollar Clubs. He attended the Company's Honor Million Dollar Conferences for twelve years running and received the Insurance's "Key Award" four times. He was the recipient of the company's Quality Award yearly for twenty years and was recognized with a National Award from the National Life Insurance Achievement Award **NINE** different times. Wow! He was Treasurer of the Local Life Underwriters and was a Centurion of the Tilt and Sword Honorary Organization. Obviously, he has received many prestigious Insurance Awards over a thirty-five year period. What a community asset.

In conclusion, he looks like your friendly neighbor, but being the super salesman that he is, hang on to your billfold with both hands or it will be much lighter after your negotiations are over!

CHAPTER 6

Village Grounds

Our supper hour is an important social time for most retirees as they will be dining and visiting with friends and neighbors. The soft murmur of the many voices rising quietly above the dining room is a comforting backdrop to the evening's repast. Here the events of the day are cussed and discussed. As time passes, most folks tend to fall into the common pattern of sitting and eating with some of the same people as a matter of convenience and friendly comfort.

Most newcomers go through a process of general acceptance. When a new resident arrives he, she, and/or they are frequently are seen eating by themselves or are escorted to empty table spots with other residents by the Maitre d'. As time passes, one or more of the permanent residents tend to drop by and join them. Soon, a number of acquaintances have been made. Many of the residents go out of their way to make newcomers feel welcome. Acceptance is an evolutionary process with no particular time lines utilized.

If one looks at the area just outside the dining room at mealtime, the sight is one to behold. The mass of walkers and scooters is amazing, and it resembles a crowded parking lot. Bringing the walkers into the dining room is frowned upon as there isn't that much room for the servers to maneuver amidst the many tables. This congestion interferes with the timely serving of warm food. This congestion has grown greatly during my past three years here by the noticeable increase in walkers and scooters.

I was amazed how many folks have fallen down and been severely injured while living here during my short time in residing at Lakeside. Some falls were very seriously injured necessitating hospitalization and or surgery.

The fear of falling is a real one for all of us. I use a walker to steady my gait at the tender age of ninety-one. There are sessions given for improving one's balance. The walker makes me feel more secure even though I could hobble along with a cane. Why take a chance? I, also, utilize my walker in getting around my apartment just for the same safety sakes. Most falls occur in the resident's apartment. My apartment walker pathways are clear and distinct. I keep a smaller and lighter walker in the trunk of my car for convenience sake when visiting stores. When my oldest son was here recently, he video taped me with my walker versus a cane. The results were eye opening and very impressive; hence, my more extensive use of the walker.

My apartment has one of the best views in this entire complex. I overlook my beautiful kingdom with its spacious manicured grounds extending downward to a good sized lake with its three large spraying fountains. The are several long, beckoning, and winding walkways waiting to be used as well as the inviting gorgeous flower gardens which complete this picture..

Lake and Fountains

When it is dark, the lake fountains are alight creating a lovely vista. The string of nearby street lights along with the various lights lining the walkways reflect onto the lake creating an illusion of a string of pearls. It is an idyllic scene. This scenario is so easy on the eyes. In the distance, the mall neon signs show forth with their reds and many other varied colors.

In the spring, summer, and early fall, it is so nice and peaceful to sit on my porch and enjoy this lovely view. There are the long, beckoning, and winding walkways which invite a person to come and stroll. My loyal subjects, the ubiquitous Canadian geese, are ever present in large number, especially during the winter months. They carry forth with their croaking and honking off and on during the night. There a large number of lazy geese who would rather winter here rather than undergo the major rigors of flying further south to the warmer climes or to go to the north for nesting purposes in the spring.

As I sit here writing this tome in late April to August 2014, the Flowering Bartlett Pears are blooming, and the Red Bud and Flowering Crabs trees are just starting to flower. The grounds are lovely with all the masses of colors on exhibition. The flowers are beginning to raise their sleepy heads to bloom and adorn the gardens with their riotous colors once more. Every Thursday, the silence is broken by the speeding lawn mowers which fill the air with the sweet odor of freshly cut grass.

There are masses of Iris with their spectacular lavender colorful petals and bearded pistils. These are beautiful to behold. There are different flowers showing their colorful wares with the changing seasons.

These flower gardens bring back memories of our backyard patio with its two large bird fountains, hanging flower baskets, and flowering tubs overflowing with blooms that my Beloved Mary diligently planted every spring. Every morning, I could hear her singing to her flowers while watering them. The flowers outdid themselves in endeavoring to bloom prettily for Mary. There were several families of beautiful brilliant red cardinals who vied singing at their loudest with her. She so loved her patio and cardinals for forty years. We had built our house in 1954.

Mary enjoyed watching the antics of the different birds fluttering around the birdbaths during the summer and vying with each other to eat at many bird feeders in our back yard during the wintertime. She was enthralled watching her many feathered friends. The picture window in our den acted as a nice bird blind from which to watch their antics.

There is a Gazebo just outside the back Village entrance with a small pond with a flourishing seven stream fountain. These streams of water dance and sparkle their way into the pool. Their ever expanding ripples, caused by this fountain's jets, journey to the far reaches of the pond. There are two bubbling outlets elsewhere just beneath the surface to keep stirring the water in order to keep it fresh.

In addition, there are two man-made water falls on a slope which are adjacent to the fountain. Their waters tumble over the rocks murmuring sweet sounds of soothing music until they fall into the pool. The pool contains cat tails and beautiful water lilies dressed in rosy reds, bright cheerful yellows, and pastoral white hues. The banks are covered with a blanket of day lilies clothed in various shades of red, orange, and yellow along with a hedge background of masses of lavender spirea bushes. This area is very picturesque and is soothing to a troubled mind whenever one takes the time to sit and absorb the peaceful tranquility.

Gazebo Pond Fountain and Waterfalls

In the early morning hours, the sun peeps its saucy head over the horizon painting the sky and the fleecy white clouds with beautiful red, pink, and orange streaks from its color palate. It is a lovely sight for sleep filled eyes to enjoy at the start of a new day.

There is adjacent to the Gazebo a broad patio, which is dressed with white umbrella tables and heavy chairs which beckon one to stop for a moment, relax, and enjoy many past memories. The patio is surrounded by day lilies of different hues and lasting blooms. There are bright sunny yellows, soft rosy reds, eye appealing pinks, and startling white blooms to admire and enjoy. This expansive patio, is used for many outdoor activities such as the "Jazz on the Green" and "Grandparent's Day" events. These events entail cotton candy, music, wine, and cheeses while participants visit and gossip with one another. Some folks might even be seen dancing! Heaven forbid!

Entrance to the Village and Flowers

Gazebo with Umbrella Tables and Chairs

Whenever there are outside activities on this lovely patio and/or lawn, my balcony serves as a front row throne to view the festivities. I can see and enjoy all the activities without leaving my royal chair.

My Balcony and Royal Throne Room

My Vast Estate from the Royal Throne Room

Just a short while ago, I was able to successfully lobby for an additional bench to be placed upon the other side of the wooden bridge on the winding walkway to the lake. This bench is a convenient rest stop when coming up or going down the incline to the lake.

This spring a sturdy pagoda is being built, which previously covered the first of the many benches on this trip to the lake. This pagoda is a replacement for the one that was blown away. A vigorous storm blew its pieces far and wide; some of which landed in the north parking lot. This catastrophe happened just a few years ago. This event was wrought by a very angry wind.

I have pushed for climbing roses or other ever blooming vines to encompass this pagoda. The erection of this new Pagoda happened just this spring. At this writing, there are a number of Honeysuckle Vines gracing the lattice work of the pagoda awaiting the opportunity to climb to the top.

These many and varied areas are pleasant places outdoors to pause, rest, and day dream awhile. As of this moment of writing, the new Pagoda is alive and well. As my own contribution to this Pagoda project, every Monday after lunch, I proceed to the Pagoda to tie up and train the vines to spread evenly across the latticework. I visit with these vines and tell them that we are glad that they came to live here and that they would become beautiful within a few years. I tie up the new growth onto the lattice work so the vines can intertwine into the open spaces. This is a most pleasant task for me.

The New Pagoda

There is a long glass corridor on the way to the Wellness Center, which is just alongside the dining room. Immediately outside these windows, there is a lovely row of floribunda, soft pink, ever blooming roses. These blooms lift their colorful blossoms to the sun's rays each day. When viewed from outside the windows and looking inward, there is created a sweet and pleasant sight. This vision is present all summer long for us to enjoy.

In the fall after a touch of frost, the colors of the different tress here and in the surrounding areas are dressed in brilliant yellows, reds, russet browns, and oranges. During the winter, the vast grounds are frequently covered with a blanket of white pristine snow. The new fallen snow is a wonderful picture for the eye to behold.

My next lobbying effort is being directed towards the establishment of a "Memory Garden" just down the walkway incline from the new Pagoda where some raised boxes for gardens exist at this present time. Many boxes have already been moved to a more convenient location for those who tire going up and down the incline. The new location of these boxes is near the Wellness Center on the south side of the facility. However, before these boxes can be effectively utilized, there needs to be a better walking surface around these areas. It is very difficult to push a walker through the grass in order to obtain a comfortable closeness to the individual garden areas.

Some progress is being made towards the proposed "Memory Garden". At least, the "Garden" is now on the priority list even though it is next to last on the very bottom of the totem pole. The names of those folks, who have gone to greet their Maker from here, could be listed by their year of departure. It would be so pleasant and convenient to sit and dream of the past years with one's beloved soul mate. There is such a "Memory Garden" at the Lauritzen Gardens, but only for those buried by a specific mortuary. My Beloved Mary is listed here. This Garden area is located so far from here that it is impossible to reach without a car. The trip is such a long drive through much traffic to access these Gardens that a journey like this is not very practical. Ipso facto! A close by Memory Garden would be the ideal solution. In addition, not everyone who passes on into the next life is buried by this particular mortuary.

CHAPTER 7

Tommie: The Dour Scotsman

I have already discussed the fellows, "Just Call Me Joe" and "Old Harry, A Man of Many Hats"; so let me turn the spotlight on nice, old "Tommie"

Tommie, A Dour Scotsman

He Went From Being A Telephone Pole Climber to Becoming A Mechanical Engineer

Tommie is ninety-four:

He has a tall, slender esthetic body build with an elongated Scotch Facies consisting of furrowed lines, deep crevasses, and wrinkles. His craggy face would be a portrait painter's delight. One can imagine him striding over the hillocks, brambles, heathers, and dales of the Scottish Highlands, with his Broadsword strapped to his side, a small dirk in his belt, and dressed in his lineage clan kilt with matching, long, argyle socks.

Pre-World War II

He grew up on a farm near the very small community of Bellwood, Nebraska during the depression days. He held many interesting jobs in his far dim-dark past. He has been a farm

hand, a dishwasher, and a waiter, which job lasted only for one night. He has been a draftsman, a blueprint specialist, and a Photostat operator.

He began an amazing career with Mother Bell, the former Telephone Company. He began his relationship with good old Mother Bell known as a Telephone "Grunt" - digging holes for poles. He became a Telephone Lineman climbing those great, big, tall, and intimidating telephone poles. For awhile, he was even a lumberjack.

World War II:

He entered the service as a foot soldier. He rapidly advanced to become a noncom with many men under his direction. As he was very strong willed, he had a disagreement with his commanding office and quickly reverted to being a private once again. He spent most of his overseas time in Belgium. He participated in the "Battle of the Bulge", a very critical front near the close of the War. He qualified as an expert Marksman. He won the sharpshooting award of his regiment.

He was housed on a farm near Saarbrucken, Belgium in a barn where he contacted Brucellosis as a gift from the dirty straw. While there, he placed his helmet on a chest in the bedroom of the house. A bomb exploded nearby. When he went to retrieve his helmet, there was a hole from the shrapnel about the size of his thumb right through the entire head covering and lining. Certainly, his guardian angel was beside him on this day.

Post World War II:

He resumed his affiliation with Mother Bell with many intriguing positions such as: Telephone Installer-repairman and being a Construction Supervisor with a four man crew. He has been a Telephone Toll Engineer, a Telephone Plant Engineer/Building Engineer, and a District Manager for buildings

His additional endeavors included being a surveyor while working in South Dakota, dabbling in architecture, electrical engineering, mechanical engineering, structural engineering, and forensic engineering.

Somewhere along the Line he has been involved in:

Being a mason-brick layer, a carpenter, and a cabinet maker. He was an electrician, a plumber, and a painter, as the builder of his own home all by himself. He accomplished these feats from scratch by his own two hands and ten little fingers. You name it, he has been there and done that. He really is a Jack-of-all-Trades.

Hobbies and Associated Activities:

He has been a small private plane pilot. He tried crop dusting, but it was not his cup of tea. He has been an ardent golfer, and a master fisherman. He was a machinist and carefully hand crafted the parts for model train engines. Believe it or not, he was a **"Masseur"**, a switchboard operator, a farm manager, and an auto mechanic. He was the sand lot pitcher for his home town, and last but not least, a "Pugilist" Wow! He has hands the size of a whole ham. What a wallop he could deliver. Man oh Man! What a Man! He and his friend, "Harry – another pitcher, frequently rehash ballgames and types of pitches thrown while they have are eating supper ad nauseam. Ugh!

What an interesting and versatile life he has led.

CHAPTER 8
The Many Different Residents

There is a dynamic young lady of about 102 years of age, who dashes around The Village on her scooter like time is of an essence. She flies into the Wellness Center, hops on the two step exercise machine; then, quick as a wink, she is back onto her scooter. Off to the Computer station she sails to make her daily birthday cards for any inhabitants, who may have turned another page of life. She drives that scooter like an Indianapolis 500 race driver. Heaven help you if you get in her way. She demands her own right-of-way – Gangway or else!

She enjoys a dip and splashes in the heated Wellness pool. Her dress is always well coordinated. I, especially, like her in pink best of all. What a woman!! If only, I could be that spry when I am at her tender age. She certainly is the "Grand Dame" of Lakeside Village!

Many of the residents decorate their doors with colorful wreaths and other items. Many inhabitants have a small stand by their door where they place figurines and other decorative items. As I walk along the halls, I enjoy observing these different concoctions and colors. Some folks change their offerings with the seasons. My Beloved Mary always wanted a seasonal wreath graced with imitation birds on our door. I have followed her dictates to this very day. In fact, I just purchased a new Thanksgiving Wreath as it is that time of the year.

There are many inhabitant Volunteers who add assistance to the carrying out of the variety of activities here at Lakeside. For example, there is "Handy Sandy", who directs his own Church Choir and our Village Choir. He sees to the singing of "Happy Birthday" to a lucky resident, who has turned another page of life onto another year. What a contribution of time and effort he makes! He used to manage the United Airline Office at Epply Airport.

There is Rosie, no relationship to Rosie the Riveter. She had twelve children and a thirteenth with her husband, as she describes her family. She helps out everywhere from the religious Catholic services on Sunday mornings to participating in the different talent shows. She loves to dress outrageously in the spirit of the different special occasion. She was a crack real estate agent. What a gal!

I first met Rosie when I was drafted to sing in the Cathedral Choir many, many years ago while in Medical School. I couldn't read a note of music, but gave the effort the old college try. The choir was very short of male bodies because of the War; so I donated mine for better or worse. Probably for the worse! I participated in the choir for the three years while I was in med school. When my time was up, I could finally tell a quarter note from a half note and/or a full note. Bully me! What an accomplishment. This deed was purely coincidental. My exposure to liturgical music was amazing and extensive during those few years.

When I was very young, the good nuns gave up on me trying to teach me to play the piano just after three months. They told my Mother to save her money. Oh well, there was always a new book to read or 'Jacks" to play.

There is "Stepdad" Manny," The Man". He is a retired real estate mogul. He sold the property that this complex is built upon to the Immanuel Board of Directors many years ago. He is a retired scratch golfer. He gave up the ghost of golf because of too many aches and pains. He played baseball while at Central High School. Later on, he refereed some sports. He has such a lovely wife.

There is an "Old, Old Bubba", who sat on the Immanuel Hospital Board for eons. He knew my dear friend and almost brother, Don Erickson, the attorney whose firm has represented Immanuel for ages and ages. Bubba had been a community planner in his past life. He is a real swinger and a good jokester. He enjoys exchanging barbs with me. He has a great sense of humor. He lives below me. I try very hard to make a lot of noise to bother him; but, the walls and floors are too thick for the sounds to penetrate enough to produce the desired effect. Shucks!

Hammy and his sweet wife, Josie, was the administrator of the new Immanuel Hospital when it moved from 36th and Ames to way, way north on 72nd Street. I had really admired Sister Ingeborg, who was the previous Immanuel Hospital Administrator, when I was very active on this medical staff.

When she retired, Hammy took her place in a very competent and professional manner. Hammy had a good vision for the future. He was responsible for establishing one of the first retirement communities in Omaha and added an outstanding rehabilitation facility to the Immanuel Hospital Campus. He was an exceptional administrator. When the land was purchased for this complex, he was way ahead of his time. I have known him for fifty some years.

When the hospital moved to far north Omaha, I retired from working at Immanuel very often. It was too time consuming to travel to and fro because of its far out location. I was active on too many different hospital staffs as it was. If you were on any active medical staff, it was required that one **MUST** attend the monthly staff meetings and participate on some of the many hospital committees. Eventually, I limited my active participation to Childrens' Hospital – my first love, Methodist, and Clarkson Hospital where I was Chief of Pediatrics for fifteen years.

At the St. Joseph, Bergan, and Immanuel Hospitals, I was on the Courtesy Staff. Being on the Courtesy Staffs was not so demanding or as time consuming. At times, if the circumstances required the need, I would become an active member on a temporary basis. There was such a need at the newly constructed Archbishop Bergan Hospital. I was asked by the Chief of the Medical Staff, Joe Gross, to head the Pediatric Department because of so many hot political headaches interfering with the department functions. I did.

I couldn't believe it. When this Hospital was built the maternity birth rate was very low in its antecedent St. Catherine Hospital. No one thought to put in an Intensive Care Nursery for premature infants and other infant special needs. This requirement had to be quickly remedied as the Maternal Delivery rate was escalating in a whirl wind fashion. When the many and various problems were resolved after three years, I resigned from the active staff and reverted to the Courtesy Staff and resigned from the Medical Staff Board.

There is old "Phillie the Farmer", who lives above me. He farmed all the different types of grains. He was a Veteran's Service Manager for eons. Everyday, he rides his "Red Racer" scooter to his garden patch down the hill to inspect, talk to, and to provide lovingly care to his tomato plants. My! He is a noisy neighbor. We enjoy bantering with each other.

There is another "Robbie" who was a nuclear physicist and worked on the atomic bomb at Los Alamos. There is such a collection of unusual folks living here. Their life stories would fill a library. This tome will barely scratch the surface.

As one would expect, there are many World War II veterans living here. "Stormie" was part of General Patton's Third Army, and was wounded in the Battle of the Bulge. He became a virologist and taught at the Med Center until his retirement. We rehash old times and many colleagues we knew over breakfast on many occasions. His lovely wife, Bertie, was a fellow Virologist at the Med Center. She is a special lady.

"Smackie", a Bomber Navigator, is a great dancer in the image of Arthur Murray. He flew twenty-six missions over Germany; and, then, was transferred to Sweden. While there, he flew as the Lead Navigator in those huge C47's, freight carrying planes to drop supplies to insurgents fighting against the Nazis located near the Arctic Circle. To guide the planes to the defined destination was a major task as failure to provide the supplies on target would only help the Nazis.

Many, many moons ago, he went to Benson High when Mary McNamara was the principal of the school. I am sure that he had several after hour punishment duties to serve while at Benson. After the War, he went to Iowa State University and became a Mechanical Engineer. He worked as a Project Manager in the Heating and Air Conditioning field.

When we have dances here, he is a regular "Fred Astaire" and cuts a mean rug. Ha! Facetiously, I call him "Twinkle Toes", and he retorts by calling me "Knobby Knees" because of my knee surgeries. It is rather pleasant way to cajole with the various people here. My own dancing days are long gone without my Beloved Mary. Dancing with her was like dancing with a feather. She was so light on her feet.

Another "Robbie" was a Bomber Pilot. He flew many German missions during World War II. He keeps the Village daily activity schedule in his shirt pocket in order know which of the many activities offered for that particular day he wants to attend..

There is " Johnno", who was a science teacher in the Lincoln Public Schools. He is another dedicated dancer at the various parties we have celebrating the different holidays. His autobiography, which "hangs it all out", is in the our Village Library. Every-so-often, he pounds loudly on the various doors with a large tub of delicious popcorn.

There are many Korean War Veterans here. There is Sworty, who was a small planes pilot. He flew his plane at low altitudes to observe and direct artillery fire. He became a big, big earth moving equipment entrepreneur and lived in North Platte and Grand Island. He was responsible for moving a great deal of Nebraska dirt of all types from here to there and back again. My! The cost of those machines is horrendous. He is a special fellow. Don't tell him that I said so; once again, he is a very lucky man as he has a lovely wife.

There is "Maggie", who is tall and willowy. She keeps abreast of all the recent changes in the political arena and otherwise. "Maggie" has a Doctorate in Education and taught Human Resources in the Millard School System. She had some relationships with the Med Center, especially, when some foreign visiting physicians appeared.

"Thea" was an intimidating and very efficient Nurse from Harlan, Iowa. She was so authoritative that she could scare any patient under her care into doing what was needed. She reminds me of "Mother Mason" of my internship days who ran the Men's Ward B at the University Hospital with an iron hand. "Thea" worked for and with many of the doctors in the Harlan, Iowa area, who referred umpteen patients to me. Both of these ladies, "Maggie" and "Thea" have the aura of extreme competence and being highly motivated in their chosen field.

With my former big consultative practice, I had many referrals from up and down the Nebraska-Iowa Missouri River seaboard and had some patients referred from as far away in communities near Des Moines, in central Iowa. I used to travel to Denison, Iowa in the mornings and, then, stop at Harlan, Iowa in the afternoons on the way home to do consultative work on the third Tuesday of the month.. This operation was of great convenience to the patients and local physicians. Due to an unnecessary change in the insurance coverage in Iowa and with a huge increase in premiums, this service had to be discontinued. It was impossible to continue this convenience due to the huge increase in malpractice insurance cost factors, which made it completely unprofitable..

This missal would not be complete without mentioning " Ouchie Smucchie", who lived in a modern sized town north of Omaha. She taught middle school, high school, and college math. She was a fearsome teacher who brooked no nonsense in her classroom. Her husband was an administrator at the local University. She has a friendly and winning disposition. She tolerates my nonsensical teasing. She lives for "Bridge". She knows my long time friend, Sherrie Murphy, whose parents were some of our very closest and dearest friends. Sherrie's Mother, Marie, was close as a sister to my Beloved Mary. While Sherrie's husband was in Dental School, I took care of the Murphy clan before they settled and further increased in size and numbers in Norfolk, Nebraska.

There is a group of ladies who have breakfast frequently together. The "Goofer" lady deluxe, who eats at this particular table, is "No Nonsense Hazzie". She use to hit the golf links three or four times a week. She claims to be a low scorer; but, I wonder if she keeps her own tally and doesn't forget a few strokes here and there.

Because of a recent car accident she had to take a hiatus from her golf. She had two broken legs which needed to be repaired with nickel plates and screws. This action caused her to have a major withdrawal episode which is just now beginning to resolve. Now that she has healed, she is champing at the bit to get back on the links.

Hazzie had five children. She has a lawyer – how sad, a doctor, two mechanical engineers, and a daughter, physical therapist with her own business. Her children have done very well under her tutelage, guidance, and direction.

Being a staunch Democrat, I enjoy teasing her just to get a rise out of her. She defends herself very well and gives back almost as good as she gets. We kibitz quite a bit. I really like her a lot and enjoy getting her goat. Shhhh! Don't tell anyon

There are a number of gardeners here who love to putter in the dirt of the raised garden boxes. "Lulu" was one such confirmed digger of the soil. She would sell her mouth watering produce to we, the residents; and, then, donate her proceeds to the scholarship fund for the graduating seniors. Unfortunately, her aching bones caught up with her and had to retire from her first love of gardening. She had been a tight fisted school teacher and farm girl. Whew! I just missed another strict teacher.

Speaking of the Scholarship Fund which started here as the first one amidst the Immanuel Retirement groups, the various folks living here at the Village donate to this fund for the graduating senior servers. "Arturo" is the Chairman of the Committee which administers this fund. He rules this committee with an iron hand. This year, 2014, $23,000 was collected. The funds were distributed to the ten graduating servers based upon the length of time and the hours spent working here. The fund is divided into parcels and is given directly to the particular school or institution in which the server has elected to attend and is enrolled in their particular choice. It helps to defray the obscene costs of attending college or other forms of higher education of their choice.

We had a graduation ceremony recently on May 20, 2014. There were ten graduates, all dressed in their finery, this year. Oh My! Each student had to be interviewed by the committee, write a one page essay on their experiences here, and come to the party with their parents. The letters were so touching as what they had received from the residents while serving us. There was some pleasant entertainment by some of the graduates.

This celebration was most enjoyable. "Sammie" played the piano. "Kathie, a graduate from last year's group, who attends Creighton University in Pre-Med, sang. She has a beautiful voice and sang such a touching song that it brought tears to my tired, old eyes. She comes back frequently on her free time to be a server. Some of the servers have a hard time leaving us as we bid them goodbye to go forth into the cold, cruel world to try their wings.

Six of the ten graduates in this year's group plan to go into some form of medicine. Don't blame me! Each recipient is called to the podium to receive their award and to say a few words to us. Their remarks are quite touching and poignant as are their essays. This ceremony completed a lovely night. We met their parents for ice cream and cake after all the hullabaloo was over. The young folks are so bright, wholesome, and industrious. They, all, participate in some type of their school's many activities.

Kasey, the Dining Room Manager, acts as the "Mother Superior" for these young folks. She trains and counsels them in public relationships and in the art of serving. She has some thirty to forty workers on her roster and under her wing in order to cover the various dining areas. These areas consist of the Independent Living, Assisted Living, and the Lighthouse with its two Skilled Nursing Sections. This large number of students is needed for serving the many residents. As each student has obligatory school requirements and as they engage in the many of the different school academic or sport activities offered, therefore, the need for so many students.

It is so enjoyable to visit with our servers while they are working at our table. We have a different one each night. We tease them and inquire about their activities, school, and related items. I eat with a group of very nosey fellows. We give the different servers a hard time as to whether or not if they drew the short straw and were coerced into handling our table. Dinner is one of the high spots of the day. The servers add a wonderful dimension to our living here.

As one can tell, there is such a diversity of people and occupations living here. One of the more interesting inhabitants is a retired newspaper reporter and editor," Jungle Slimmy". He taught journalism on the West Coast for awhile and was on our local Omaha World Herald newspaper staff as a reporter and as an editor. It is a pleasure to visit with him at lunch rather frequently and enjoy teasing him all in fun. He has a son, who is a noted author and lives in England.

I am constantly impressed with the variety of disease processes residing here amongst the residents. In some ways, it is a virtual medical museum. Some folks have multiple problems, but handle them without much complaining. This population is a paradise for the Pharmacists, Internists, and the Geriatricians, who deal with our age bracket.

The medical situations range from lymph edema in the arms, to swollen ankles from heart failure, to renal dialysis three times per week, and/or to post stroke residual rehabilitation. There is a plethora of macular degeneration, cataracts, and glaucoma amidst the individuals living here. Many, many of the residents need hearing assistance of some type. Rarely do you hear anyone complain or go into hibernation.

I have been spared many of these different maladies so far. The way these folks cope with their disabilities is heartwarming and is a lesson in and of itself. There are many joint replacements among us including both of my knees. These individuals are source of inspiration to those of us with fairly good health. There are many folks who have had open heart surgery of one type or another. Four of the five fellows at our supper table have had such procedures. One of these had an aortic aneurysm which was removed; and a prosthesis was inserted in its place. He is very lucky that it had not ruptured before it was found. If so, it would have been "Lights Out".

There is NO evidence of "Warehousing" here. Everyone is too active and interested in living a vigorous and fruitful life. Once again, the staff pays close attention to our Mind, Body, and Spirit. It works wonders.

"Avie" is one of these most unusual folks. She is a walking and scooter riding medical text book with lymph edema of her arm, heart problems, and various other maladies.

She has traveled far and wide in her lifetime from Asia to Florida. Her husband graduated from Annapolis. Because of Navy regulations, they had to wait until he graduated from the Academy before marrying. They had the inspiring "Saber Arch" upon on leaving the Chapel. He was a flier in the original United States Air Corp before the Navy Air force came into being. She was a brilliant math teacher, is an avid bridge player, and handles a computer like a skilled technician. She taught math in elementary school, high school, and college.

"Daffie" is a well rounded "Irish Mic" who went through the bombing of the Island of Malta during World War II. She was married to a Brigadier General, who is buried at West Point. She has traveled far and wide from Ireland to Germany; thence, onward to Hong Kong. She had four sons who are lawyers. We will try hard not to hold that against her and has two other sons doing something else. A great and friendly gal with a smile for everyone – even little old me. She has such a gift of gab that she must have kissed the Blarney Stone on several different occasions.

There are a number of people, whose children I was privileged to care for, who are living here. My pediatric practice contained a plethora of wonderful families. I was a very fortunate physician.

There is "Deanie Beanie" who owned a number of mortuaries with her husband from and near Broken Bow, Nebraska. Due to the area's needs, they operated an emergency ambulance service as a sideline for several counties.

She grew up in Oklahoma and picked cotton as a young child. She played basketball in high school and was a one woman coaching staff in her home town. She coached softball and swimming and is one dynamic lady who walks the halls at least twice a day religiously, like a marathon walker in training. Four of her children have gone into medicine with three doctors, and one nurse. Wow! She has a daughter in her sixty's who plays Professional Volleyball in an International League.

Miz Irish Lurleen drives her scooter like she was another race driver. For some silly reason or another, she lives to play bridge. She would rather play cards than eat. Every Monday, she is the first to arrive at the tables and the last one to throw in the cardboards. She had six children – two physicians and two lawyers. Alas for the lawyers!

Her father and brother were outstanding physicians. Her father was a small town practitioner. Her brother, Emmet, was one of the first and really good common sense Adolescent Psychiatrists in Omaha. I used him on many occasions after he began practicing here. Before that, I needed to become my own pseudo-makeshift psychiatrist due to an obvious lack of sensible psychiatrists who were not Freudian based. Those Freudian followers wouldn't know an Ego" from an "Id" in children and adolescents if it jumped up and bit them when it came to the real world of practicality..

There is "Bett", with whom I eat lunch frequently. She has an excellent bright mind, a very sharp tongue, graduated from South High School, and has always lived in Omaha. Her husband worked for good old "Mother Bell". One of her children is a Minister in Lincoln. She has a daughter, who is in finances and is a Trust Officer for a prominent bank.

She has a granddaughter, who was a graduated dinning room server and just finished her four year Nursing Degree. She passed her Nursing Boards with a flourish and was recently hired by the new Women's Methodist Hospital. She has achieved her first love on the hospital nursing staff by being assigned to caring for ICU infants. We had to bid a tearful goodbye.

There is a group of us who frequently gather for lunch around a table meant for four, but a total of eight have been noted to congregate and crowd in. Table corners are used as places to sit and have a bite. The world and local gossip frequently are the subjects for conversation. The world's problems are solved at this congregation.

"Kayloulou", the noon Dining Room Supervisor, would rather that we sit four to a table for serving convenience; but, that arrangement is not nearly as enjoyable as eight. She thinks that "I am "Irritating" and "Ornery" for wanting to eat with the larger number." How could that be? Certainly not little old me!"

There is "Berry", the Navy Swab, who is an ex-submariner. He had two brothers in the Army, who told him to join a different branch of the Services; so he become a Navy man. He has sailed the seven seas on seven different submarines and back again and has multiple tattoos [40+] to show for his love of the Navy. How he avoided HIV from the tattooing I'll never know.

He was a communication specialist whose job was to listen for clandestine signals. His sub identified a brand new Russian Sub. They stayed very quiet, observed, and studied this Sub off Russia for quite awhile. His own was never identified by the Russians. He was aboard both diesel and nuclear subs.

He was a twenty year navy man. While in the Navy, he shipped aboard two Air Craft Carriers. He had different shore duties in Norfolk, Virginia and Japan and is an avid pinochle player.

"Old Helpful Moey" has a wonderful, bright daughter with whom I had worked when I was the Medical Advisor for a software company. She and Lynne E. were two of the smartest ladies I have ever encountered. Old "Moey" is busy, busy doing various tasks around here and volunteering for many jobs everywhere. He is a jack of all trades and a great guy.

There is "Buddy, Old Buddy Boy Dwayne". During World War II, he joined the Naval V12 Program and went to flight school. He was shipped here and there in the States to many different training schools. Nearing the end of his training, he was told by the Navy that it had too many pilots so they said to him "Sayonara".

After the war, he started out as a Mother Bell Pole Climber. He is another North High Alumni and graduated the year behind me. Naturally, he is much, much older than I am. Mother Bell sent him to South Dakota and thence on to Alaska on two different occasions. Too bad, he saw fit to return to the Lower States. He is a gifted wood carver and has many finished birds to plead his case. He is a dedicated Shrine member and acts as a "Shrine Greeter" for special Shrine occasions along with several other friends of mine from North High School. He had a great wife. I was privileged to care for his family.

There is generous "Reenie", who donated a brand new sixteen passenger bus to our complex. It replaced the tired, old, old moth eaten version which made all kinds of noise. It rattled your teeth whenever a bump was encountered. It had terrible shock absorbers. Many "Thanks" to you "Reenie"! She always dresses so very well, grew up near Holdrege, Nebraska, and lived in Washington D.C. for many years. She is a very nice lady.

There is "New Jersey Freddie", who just moved into our habitat. He is an interesting fellow. He was in the Signal Corps during WW II and was an executive in the Information Technology Field. He grew up in Svedberg, which is a small spot on the road in outstate Nebraska. He lived in New Jersey for seventy years before migrating back to Omaha and the good life..

There is Robbie, a lovely lady, who lived for years in California. She is the world's best visitor and can talk on forever. Her husband, Dannie, was a "Wheel" with the Union Pacific Railroad in charge of any "Toxic Spills". He related an episode about having to fly experts from Texas to a specific bad spill as there were no knowledgeable people closer to the site. It was a pleasure to have him address various aspects of Railroading. I was privileged to care for their family.

There is Ellie, who was married to a very prominent Omaha Lawyer. She was a "Wesley Girl" and came from the East. She met her husband, who was a Harvard Law Graduate, while in school. He came from Omaha; so they returned here to live and practice law.

CHAPTER 9

"Dick"
The Indispensible Man

"Is there a town in South Dakota that He Hasn't Lived-in"

Dick was an Amoco Executive in South Dakota. He was born in 1930 in Madison, South Dakota and was raised there.

Young Dick:

He was born left handed and tried to change handedness without much success, later on he broke his left arm and tried, in vain, to use his right hand. Very early on he had Dyslexia, but subsequently overcame this handicap. He has a large physique with too much hair with steel graying streaks sneaking throughout it. He must have been a handsome Dude in his dim dark past. His son is the spitting image of him. They could almost pass for twins.

His father died when he was seventeen years old. During high school and beyond, he had many different jobs ranging from working for a Sand and Gravel Company, which pumped sand out of the pits. Starting at the tender age of fourteen, he helped to separate the many different grades of sand. He drove a huge sand truck without as a license as there was no need for one as young as fourteen in South Dakota. Watch out you, drivers! He worked in a movie theatre as an usher and then, as a projectionist off and on for several years.

College Years:

He went to the South Dakota State College at Madison, South Dakota, where he studied Mechanical Engineering for two years.

War Years:

He joined the Navy during the Korean War and served as a Diesel man aboard an Attack Transport Ship that carried one thousand two hundred [1200] Marines and three hundred and fifty [350] sailors aboard. This ship practiced amphibious landings in the Mediterranean and onto several islands in the Caribbean ocean. They used twenty-six [26] LCD Landing Crafts for their exercises. These Crafts were carried aboard this vessel in addition to the crew and troops.

While in the Mediterranean area, he visited many cities. Amongst his many valorous adventures, he climbed the Rock of Gibraltar. There were many, many macaque monkeys playing on the Rock. He attended Christmas Services in a small Protestant Church. The church was packed for the Christmas services..

In 1953, he had a four day leave and went to Rome where he joined a Tour. He saw the Sistine Chapel, St. Peter's Church, and Pope Pius XI; and, he also, journeyed to Southern France enjoying the Riviera and Monte Carlo. He insists that he did **NOT** do any gambling. Ha! Want to bet?

1954:

His time in the service ended, and returned to South Dakota. He became the Service Manager for a Pontiac-Cadillac Dealership. He married his High School Sweetheart in 1955 and drove to Huron, South Dakota to the Standard Oil Division Office for a job interview, where he was hired.

After driving to Brooking, South Dakota to the Standard Oil Training facility, he was a salesman for two years and lived in Brooking another two years, where his son was born.

In 1957, the Standard Oil Company cut the Sales Force **in** half. He was promoted to District Analyst and was, subsequently, transferred to Mitchell, South Dakota as the Territory Manager. His daughter, Julie-a very special lady, was born in 1961. He bought a house; and then, had to sell it on very short notice because he was being transferred once more to Aberdeen, South Dakota. He was the District Trainer for South Dakota and half of North Dakota for two years.

After the transfer to Rapid City, South Dakota as the Sales Manager, he supervised six salesmen in this position. He moved to Minneapolis for an interview and managed the Sales Training for North and South Dakota, Minnesota, and Wisconsin Territories and did not have to travel nearly as much with this position..

He developed a Dealer Replacement Training Center to help prospects learn how to manage a Service Station. When this office was closed, he was moved to Cedar Rapids, Iowa as the Senior Sales Manager.

In 1968, he began selling fertilizer and agriculture chemical products, subsequently, was promoted as the Kansas City Manager, which was a part of Standard Oil. He remained there four years and lived in the prestigious Overland Park Area. Subsequently, he was transferred to Albert Lee, Minnesota and handled a large Farm Store that offered many agriculture chemical products. This change was deemed a lateral move in the management hierarchy.

In 1975, he handled fertilizer plants and seven Territorial Managers. Later in 1975, he came to Omaha, Nebraska where he became a Sales Manager, once again. He retired in 1986.

With all of these moves, his dear wife became a moving artist and specialist. When she received notice of a needed move, the house was packed and on its way within the wink of an eye. She was able to quickly locate her desired neighborhood, new church, and school for their children. This packing and moving became a second nature to her. Nothing seemed to phase her. Dick was a very fortunate man.

His dear wife and life companion died in 1997 after being married for forty-two years. She succumbed to the notorious "Lou Gehrig Disease". She needed to utilize a chairlift in her house in her later years due to her disabilities.

John and his beloved wife took many trips together. After her demise, John stayed in his house until 2009 when he moved into the Immanuel Lakeside Village Complex.

He was quite a golfer until he experienced macular degeneration, which has limited his activities. He is a marvelous, bright man with a sly wit. He has a wonderful daughter and a special daughter-in-law, who look after him with a no nonsense eagle eye.

CHAPTER 10
Some Friendly Neighbors

The Immanuel Village Support Staff is outstanding. "Sammie", the manager of the Life Services, has been here for at least a hundred years. "Lucella", alias "Lulu", a former Social Worker used to be a part of the Lighthouse Staff until this move to the Life Services area. These ladies provide the knowhow and manpower for all of our various endeavors. Meggie just joined them and seems to fit right into their midst. She is a very pleasant person, has a nice personality, and is my newest heart throb along with these other two special people. Ha!

This group of ladies frequently drive the bus for the "Blue Brothers" monthly luncheon outings. By consensus, we, the men, decide where we will go the each month. These special ladies are a real "Hoot" when they are with us, and we tease them unmercifully. They seem to enjoy our shenanigans and keep coming back for more. The number of men going to the luncheons ranges from five or six to ten or twelve. There are about seventeen or more restaurants that we enjoy. These wonderful ladies make this a very enjoyable outing.

The Activities Staff does a magnificent job of planning for the holidays, the programmed special events, and for "The Traditional Social Hour" on Fridays, where they exchange their Management Hats for those of being Bar Maids. They are full of life, fun and add zest to our lives.

These lovely women have many activities for us to attend. Some of these have been a trip to the local Werner Professional Ballpark to watch the Storm Chasers play or to the Discount Mall in Nebraska City where I snooped through the Van Huesen store and purchased a beige sweater and a tan, long sleeved shirt. There was a trip to the huge Nebraska Crossing Mal on the highway to Lincoln, Nebraska with its multiple new shops, and an excursion to our sister installation, "The Landing", in Lincoln. This trip was one of our more pleasant outings. The Landing is very nice, but our place is so much better. Ha! We had a great luncheon.

I have given two book review readings to the folks at the Landing. I revisited with some former patients of mine, who reside there, all the while I was blatting to them. As a very pleasant surprise for me, two former Servers from the Village, who, now, work at the Landing while going to the University of Nebraska at Lincoln, came to see me; and each one gave me a great big hug. Wow! What a tasty treat!

At Christmas time, these Activity Ladies arrange for Christmas Light Tours within the city. It seems as though there always is some new or different adventure hiding up their sleeves

Lucella, "Lulu", supervises the Transportation Department. "Legs" Reggie and "Dellie the Melliel" are the accommodating drivers of the cars. They either drive the cars or the bus for trips to doctor appointments, to the grocery store, and to Wal-Mart. Friday is special drop-off day. They take us and pick us up everywhere we need to go within our outlined boundaries. We feel safe and sound with them at the wheel. When my Beloved Mary was in the Skilled Nursing Section undergoing rehab, these friends drove us to her doctor appointments and waited until we were done. They are very solicitous of us.

Marcus is the overall chief mogul and bottle washer of the Village. He is a very experienced coordinator of this active complex with a very long, long resume. He has his hands full with his administration chores and with coordinating the needs of almost two hundred of we, the residents. Trouble shooting, hiring and firing, attending to client needs and complaints, going to umpteen meetings, and a host of other tasks, all, fall under his purview. He has an excellent background and insight for this job as his Father was a small town Family Practitioner during the depression days.

He wears some of the most "horrendous" ties that you have ever seen. We exchange friendly bantering and teasing at frequent intervals. He has an important major job and role in being in compliance with public health mandates whenever there is a "Flu" or other outbreak within the City; besides all of these matters, he needs to provide for the expert handling of the budget of this magnificent complex. A successful Retirement Center is a very serious big business. From my perspective, being an old Public Health advocate, he does a great job whenever a health problem rears its ugly head. Shhhh! Don't tell him that I said so.

The Lakeside Village has won the Omaha Award for being **Number One** amongst the many retirement complexes within the Omaha area seemingly forever and once again in 2014.

Marcus has a lovely and gifted wife, who plays the piano beautifully. She occasionally gives us a taste of her talents over the supper hour and has a winning and very friendly personality.

Fortunately for Marcus, he has a very able assistant in "Fancy Nanny", who, also, has been here since the beginning of time. She keeps an eagle eye on the finances and is in charge of the Christmas decorations. Our complex literally becomes a fairy land during the holiday season. She saw to it that we tidied up our various store room spaces. She certainly is a no nonsense gal, but is especially nice.

Everything in this book would be amiss if I didn't mention Lannie and Marie in the Marketing and Rental department. They are so apt at their marketing endeavors that they could sell the very shoes off your feet while you were still in them or the gold out of your teeth. Along with the ladies in the Activities Department, they are my two special favorite people on the staff and always have a cheery hello and a great big, big smile for everyone. They are my very special Heart Throbs.

Little "Casey" at the front desk keeps the wheels of this domicile turning with her handling of the multitude of tasks and duties that she is responsible for. These duties range from supervising the daily check-ins of we, folks, to being our Postmistress and Notary Public with everything else in between. She must have ten arms and twenty hands to handle her myriad of tasks. She always has a pleasant smile for anyone, whoever comes into front office.

The maintenance folks, Christie, "Man of the Hour", and Gregor, with their assistants, keep our living wheels turning while watching out for the heat, air conditioning, apartment problems, and a plethora of other tasks. They, literally, keep the roof intact over our head. A special thanks to Gregor for his pushing for the completion of the new Pagoda. This staff is very efficient and accommodating.

I already mentioned "Pretty Henny" Penelope and "Old" Johnston of the Wellness Department. They are very dedicated to their job and to us old duffers. They are determined to see that our health stays in good shape. Johnston supervises the heated pool and Henny Penny rules, like a Chief Mogul, over the Wellness Center with all of the exercise machines. She has an iron hand in a velvet glove and a sharp eye. Woe to those who do not follow her dictates. She helped my Beloved Mary regain herself so much that she is in my daily prayers. She is one tough and demanding little lady who never walks anywhere but gallops. She teaches many different types of exercise classes.

As an aside and back in our previous civilian life before Lakeside, there were of us eight couples who would go to dinner before the Omaha Playhouse or the Omaha "Pops" concert. At one such dinner, I happened to look across the table at Le Clair, and Wow! Help! She was choking. I quietly stood up and walked behind her and administered the Hemlock maneuver. It was successful! I slowly returned to my chair, and no one was the wiser of the near tragedy. I had occasion to do the same here at Lakeside when we first arrived. Once on a lady and another time on a gentleman. As a doctor, surprise things seem to happen when least expected.

CHAPTER 11
Our Living Quarter's Decor

As I sit here pondering my next Chapter, I look out my window and see the expansive manicured grass, the trees which are in the process of covering their leafy boughs with a crown of green, and the lake with its three fountains throwing out tall sprays of water in a picturesque manner. There is a background of an azure blue sky with many floating, fleecy, white clouds. It is a quiet and peaceful scenario. The fountains in the lake along with the one in the gazebo pond are lighted up at night which makes for a peaceful portrait.

At this present time, the lily pads in the gazebo pond are blooming with their saucy yellows, rosy reds, and the angel white flowers. This small pond by the gazebo is so restful and provides a peaceful setting in which to relax during a busy day. There is the fountain bubbling along without end and the two water falls that tumble over the man made rocks while murmuring musical sounds on their way to dance in the pond.

As I sit by this water, memories from my mind's archives keep coming to the fore and playing in my mind like the repeated refrains from a song. As I was very active at the national level within the American Academy of Pediatrics for about fifteen years, Mary and I touched at least forty-eight of the fifty-two States, took nine cruises including our twenty-three day voyage to occupied Japan on a cruise ship, and a ten day trip home on the "Old Rust Bucket", the SS Sergeant Fremont. With our many cruises, we visited most of the main Caribbean Islands.

We took a tour of Southern England with Mary's sister and her husband, and our fiftieth Anniversary honeymoon was a tour of Rome. Ours has been a great life for sixty-six years. Now, I relive my memories with happiness and with great pleasure as I amble along these halls.

The interior of our habitat is very restful and homelike. The Independent Living Quarters covers three floors. Sometimes, we are so busy running nowhere and seeing nothing that we forget to stop and admire the beauty which is right before our eyes. There are longitudinal corridors stretching north on each floor from the main entrance. As I mosey along the hallways musing over my many wonderful memories with ever my busy imagination, It takes me on many different adventures from our past life with my Beloved Mary. There is a background of soft, romantic instrumental music of the 1930's 40's, and 50's drifting down from ceiling speakers to provide listening pleasure and relaxing music while strolling along.

The music is reminiscent of dancing under the stars at beautiful and romantic outdoor ballroom, the Royal Grove, at Peony Park with its myriads of fragrant peonies and other blooms. My Beloved Mary and I so enjoyed dancing as a pastime. As I have said before," Dancing with Mary was like dancing with a feather". She was so graceful. We danced during the "Smooth Dancing Era". It was great to glide along with a beautiful partner in one's arms.

While I am contemplating and wending my way along the halls, a thousand memories come flooding back to my mind. I walk these halls every Tuesday and Thursday mornings. Each of these morning walks covers three tenths of a mile. Each day is a different adventure from my memory library.

The hallways were redecorated just three years ago with new carpeting, paint, and wall paper. There are numerous decorations on the walls of the halls consisting of mirrors, and pictures. There are many inviting corners with tables and lamps. There is a different decor on each floor with restful lounges at the end of each hall.

There is a different thematic approach to each of the three floors. The end of the hall lounges are so comfortable that they beckon folks to come and sit for kibitzing, gossiping, and/or just passing the time of the day. When we lived on the third floor, my Beloved Mary and I would sit and visit in the north end lounge while our apartment was being cleaned. One finds a table for playing card games, and a long table for projects such as putting a thousand piece jig saw puzzle together in each lounge. As one walks along, there are many different jigsaw puzzles to be seen in various stages of being assembled.

The furniture is comfortable and conducive for one to stop and spend a few peaceful moments. There are end tables, containing decorative table lamps and fancy bowls filled with bouquets of beautiful artificial flowers, and interesting books residing there waiting to be perused.

There are a low coffee tables fronting the couches awaiting for visitors to place their materials which are planned to be utilized while enjoying the lounge. Everywhere you can turn, there is a convenient telephone just waiting to be picked up and used.

One can view a number of ceramic, three dimensional wall decorations. There are many different figurines gracing cabinets and shelves and lovely colorful bowls and vases of realistic artificial flowers abounding upon the various tables along with décor lamps. There are many pictures which conjure up thoughts of past adventures as I meander along.

There are copies of paintings, which are enticing one to dream, depicting restful rural scenes and several different inviting English rural lanes and meadows beckoning to come and explore. One picture, especially, keeps enticing me to come and have a peaceful amble over hills and dales through the countryside where[1] my memories can conjure up past memorable moments. Every time I view this picture, I want to go exploring along this peaceful lane and day dream with my Beloved Mary.

There is a picture of Diamond Head on the Isle of Oahu, in Hawaii which recalls our many trips to the Hawaiian Islands, especially Oahu and Maui, for meetings and vacations. I so enjoyed snorkeling. Mary would get the best laugh as she watched me clump towards the water with my big fins dangling off my feet. The best snorkeling I ever enjoyed anywhere was off the Black Rock Reef near the Sheraton Resort Hotel on the Island of Maui. I tried to be an underwater photographer, but the fish would not cooperate. They wouldn't stand still while I took their picture. With persistence, I was successful with a few shots, but not many.

While meandering, there are so many lovely thoughts which strive to come to my mind's surface in order to be relived again. One can observe a graceful Southern Mansion of the 1860's which we saw while we were in New Orleans or enjoy a visit to a French Villa on the Mediterranean Seaside. One sees many picturesque pastoral scenes which are an inducement to explore at one's leisure.

Here are beckoning seascapes with groups of moored sailing craft. In some pictures, there are active crafts with fully extended sails and are running hard on the wind while others are rocking back and forth while anchored and being impatient to go to sea. Being an old sailor, these craft recall many pleasant memories sailing a Snipe on Lake Manawa just outside of Council Bluffs, Iowa. As a family, we would water ski every Friday and sail in the Snipe and Dingy Races every Sunday. My Beloved Mary was the most graceful skier in the family.

There are colorful Mediterranean Riviera Villas and Italian sidewalk cafés inviting one to stop and partake of some refreshments and many different inviting European countryside vistas. One can easily walk the London streets in the warm rain or ride a two Decker bus. When we visited London, Mary and I walked along, hand in hand, with her sister and husband, Bob - my favorite Brother-in-Law. We took the Underground, watched the "Changing of the Guards at Buckingham Palace, strolled through Westminster Abbey with many of its historic personages, and visited the Tower of London with its Crown Jewels and marvelous collection of Medieval Armor for knights and their horses. We toured Southern England and visited with King Arthur and his Knights of the Round Table at Tintagel, Cornwall. I could imagine myself being a knight sitting at the Round Table. It is wonderful to revisit our many trips as I amble along the halls.

On another day, I can stand on a Paris Street and gaze at the Eiffel Tower or The Cathedral of Notre Dame, or enjoy a cup of coffee, a glass of wine, or cup of cappuccino at one of the many French Cafes or an Italian Palazzo café which are pictured on the walls. One can visit a French countryside villa while never having to travel overseas.

For our fiftieth wedding anniversary, my Beloved Mary and I went to Rome where we explored the many ancient ruins, gazed with awe in St. Peter's Cathedral, attended a Papal outdoor Audience with Pope John Paul, the Polish Pope. Mary's Father came from Warsaw, Poland. This was a special moment for her. We enjoyed the Fountain of Trevi and purchased a replica of the famous "Pieta". I am quite an ancient history buff and enjoyed explaining the different ruins and sights to Mary.

We took a Greek Island cruise which was wonderful. We traveled to the Island of Mikonos where the Greek Myth of the Labyrinth is and its story is located in Theses where the Minotaur dwelled. We took the cable car in lieu of a donkey ride up to the colorful city on the top of the Island of Santorini with its narrow streets and bountiful flowers everywhere.

The Island of Rhodes with its magnificent fortifications was a great favorite of mine with its history of Medieval Knights defending Christendom and Europe from the Turks. When we were in Ephesus, I had cold chills standing outside the outdoor amphitheatre where St. Paul preached. This anniversary trip was a major lifetime highlight for us.

The walls of our different halls contain many different prints and pictures depicting restful scenes, such as a countryside picture with a peaceful stream flowing through the beckoning fields, children playing in these fields, or hearing the musical sound of a waterfall as it falls into a still pool and thence into a wandering stream. One can imagine oneself lying by a babbling brook watching the white clouds float bye.

There are Amsterdam rivers and canal scenes with moored house boats on which people actually live year round. There are different fishing boats resting on placid waters waiting to be pressed into service. Rowboats with their oars impatient to be plied on lakes and streams. There is even a canoe to enjoy, which recalls the many canoe trips I took as a scoutmaster with my troop. So many still life pictures of spacious gardens inviting one to walk amidst the blooms with the sweet perfumed odors filling the air. There are people playing golf and children fishing in ponds or playing in the fragrant meadows.

My Beloved Mary so loved her backyard patio. It was so like a beautiful park. In the early mornings, she could be heard singing off key while watering her flowers and hanging baskets. The flowers would so enjoy hearing her voice that they would try extra hard to be beautiful just for her. Our old dog, "Duke" would enjoy lapping water from the hose. There were several families of cardinals which nested in our many trees. They would sing at top of their voices to accompany Mary's songs. She so loved her brilliant red cardinals.

Mary had such a sweet whimsical and sly sense of humor which surprised me on many occasions.

There are people playing golf and children playing in the fragrant meadows.

One is pleased with groups of stark bare tree trunks silhouetted against the sky, and several groves of trees in their leafy splendor. There are portraits of lovely young ladies ready to be admired.

All in all, the décor has great eye appeal. One can enjoy imagining a master violinist playing a Stradivarius before a hushed audience, or the ivory keys of a grand piano being tickled by a virtuoso while giving a wonderful concert to an enthralled audience. Just as easily, one can imagine a novice practicing her/his scales endlessly.

I remember well that there were four of us couples who went to dinner at the Omaha Club before attending the "Omaha Pops Concert" where we heard Piano and Violin Artists being featured guests to play with the orchestra.

These thoughts can be met just by day dreaming and looking at the pictures. The many lovely and different appointments makes living here a real pleasure.

There are, fortunately for me, a very, very few contemporary modernistic artistic pieces. I fail to understand or am unable to interpret whatever the artist is trying to depict in these types of paintings. Thank heavens! There are not too many of these horrendous concoctions. My meager art education fails to provide any insight for me to enjoy this type of art – if that is what it is supposed to be.

A sedate homey feeling pervades this interior ambiance. All in all, the décor is excellent. The total atmosphere here creates a lovely and peaceful domicile in which to reside.

Many nooks and crannies are scattered here and there and have chairs for visiting or stopping to rest a moment. There is a small but current library which exists off of the main entrance foyer. There is a good selection of contemporary authors where some of my own books can be found. On occasion, I'll borrow a book. Volunteers keep the books shelved and in order.

A small cozy and peaceful lounge is just across from the library with several groupings of large comfortable chairs and a large fireplace on the end wall of the lounge. During the winter months, a friendly gas log has flames dancing merrily to an inaudible tune.

There is a large gathering room just adjacent to this small lounge with comfortable living room type of chairs, end tables and complete with lamps, and wall decorations. Another large fireplace with a large impressive mantle which holds seasonal figurines at the Thanksgiving and Christmas seasons is at one end. Many different entertainment activities are held in this comfortable room. I have given four book reviews of my writings in this edifice.

Closely allied to this large assembly room is the activities room with several card tables where King Bridge is played every Monday and some evenings. Woe to the person who walks through, breaks the silence, or intrudes through this room when cards are considered the master of this universe. Pinochle assumes it rightful place when bridge is not the big inhibitor. Movies and the Nebraska Football Games hold sway here on Saturday and Sunday evenings.

The Social Bar inhabits one corner of this room. Many different types of "Adult Beverages" are distributed from this counter during the Friday Social Hour. Our cheerful Bar-maids, drafted from the Activities Office, try very hard to stock a client's favorite adult beverage. I, personally, enjoy the white German Wines, especially, "Piesporter". Many voices are raised with happy levity during these hours creating a friendly intermingling of diverse conversations.

Just outside and adjacent to this assembly room is a large inviting patio complete with black, wrought iron umbrella tables and chairs for anyone's use as desired. There are several large flower tubs which are overflowing with colorful blooms and a very large gas grill for barbecuing on special cook-out occasions.

Main Patio with Umbrella Tables and Chairs

The dining room is Casey's domain. She shepherds a group of some forty teenagers who are trained over a period of time to be friendly, experienced servers for the evening meal. Casey is their "Mother Superior" and looks out diligently for her students' interests much like a fussy "Mother Hen". These young folks work in the Assisted Living, the Light House-Skilled Nursing Section, and the main dining room. She makes allowances and provisions for their many involvements in their own school activities, family trips, and vacations. I learned that workers under fifteen years of age by Law are only allowed to work three hours per day and **MUST** be on their way home by 7:00 pm.

The meals are varied, tasty, and nutritious for our age bracket. These meals are a strong grade four gourmet experience. The repasts comprise of a selection from two appetizers such as a bowl of fresh daily made tasty soup and/or a scrimp cocktail, a daily featured salad or another one of your choice, and two ever changing main entrées, plus selected desserts and drink. Over several weeks, the menus are varied and offer an extensive selection of foodstuffs. The meals are well prepared in a spotless kitchen and presented in an inviting fashion .The Chief Chef and Bottle Washer, Mattie, wields his authoritative cleaver with a wicked hand.

All in all, this is a very pleasant place to live and social

EPILOGUE

This tour of my Beloved Mary and my activities including the folks at the Lakeside Village has come to its inevitable conclusion. Some folks may breathe a sigh of relief that my rambling comments have ended without including them. For better or worse, I have endeavored to portray my life and living here from an unbiased viewpoint. You will have to decide how close I have come.

I started this literary work in the early spring when the trees where just beginning to leaf out and the flowers beginning to bud. Now, it is fall, and the trees are beginning to turn russet browns, brilliant yellows, deep reds, and saucy orange colors. Already, many leaves have floated to the ground to await the winter snows.

This exercise has made me appreciate even more where I live and why I stayed after my Beloved Mary went home with the angels. My final joyful memories of my Mary are ensconced and intertwined in my heart here concerning her final days of pleasure and happiness .Now, if I just had the "Memory Garden", my day dreams could be complete.

When I left my apartment on the third floor, I left my ghosts behind and brought all my memories with me to my lovely apartment overlooking the lake and the beautiful grounds. Here I can and do frequently have many pleasant daydreams. I lovingly recall that Mary's last two years were made so nice while living here. What a blessing for her to have such an enjoyable end chapter to her life.

As I sit here completing this essay, contemplating, and reliving our many family outings and trips together, it is very apparent that my Beloved Mary and the Mother of our three boys was the adhesive force that made it all seem so effortless and possible. She was a unique and remarkable woman and person.

I had always prayed to be able to marry a nice Catholic girl, that she would go home to heaven before me, and that she would have a peaceful demise. My prayers were well answered over a hundred fold times.

God bless you, the Readers, and keep you from harm. Amen

Printed in the United States
By Bookmasters